BEGINNING
WORSHIP GUITAR

INSTRUCTION FOR
THE WORSHIP MUSICIAN

SANDY HOFFMAN

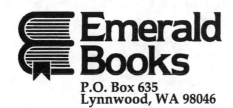
Emerald
Books

P.O. Box 635
Lynnwood, WA 98046

Emerald Books are distributed through YWAM Publishing. For a full list of titles, including other worship resources, visit our website at:

www.ywampublishing.com

Published by Emerald Books
P.O. Box 635
Lynnwood, Washington 98046

ISBN: 1-883002-72-9

Beginning Worship Guitar

DEDICATION

To my three kiddos, Lauren, Nicholas and Nathan;
the most fun (and loved) beginners I ever taught!

CONTENTS

INTRODUCTION

SECTION I. GETTING STARTED

SECTION II. THE KEY OF C MAJOR

SECTION III. THE KEY OF G MAJOR

SECTION IV. THE KEY OF D MAJOR

SECTION V. KEY OF E MAJOR

SECTION VI. MINOR KEYS

SECTION VII. ALL TOGETHER NOW!

APPENDICES

IN CLOSING

INTRODUCTION

Soon after writing the *Essential Worship Guitar* book, I came to a startling realization. In my passion to equip already established guitarists to honor the Lord with their instruments, I had totally leapt over quite an important segment of the picking population—those who were just getting started! Obviously a "prequel" was in order. The result? *Beginning Worship Guitar*.

The purpose of the *Beginning Worship Guitar* book is to prepare you, the beginning guitarist, to flow completely uninhibited from one chord to another as you worship God with your instrument.

Like *Essential Worship Guitar*, the book is laid out in seven sections. These build in a logical progression from just getting started to playing chords all together. Along the way the beginning guitarist is exposed to chord diagrams, strumming skills, major and minor keys, and time signatures. Also included are appendix items such as guitar finger board notes and the number system.

As you move prayerfully through the *Beginning Worship Guitar* book, my hope and desire is that you'll become fully equipped to use the people's instrument (the guitar) to do just as Psalm 67:3 says:

Let the peoples praise You, O God. Let all the peoples praise You!

Have fun!

Yours in Christ,

Sandy

I. GETTING STARTED

ABOUT THE GUITAR

I.   **The guitar is most commonly a 6 string instrument (though some guitars have 12 strings).**

The strings of the guitar are named **E - A - D - G - B - E**. These start with the largest, or sixth string and move downward to the smallest, or first string.

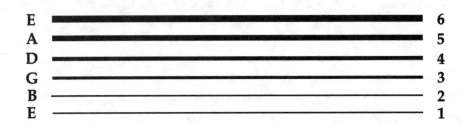

II. **The strings of the guitar are strummed with the pick, or "plectrum."**

Hold the pick firmly between the right hand thumb and index finger at a 90 degree angle to the thumb.

III. **The pick should usually glide down and up across the strings over the back third (1/3) of the sound hole.**

IV.   The closer to the bridge of the guitar the strings are
        strummed, the <u>brighter</u> the tone.

        The closer to the finger board of the guitar the strings
        are strummed, the more <u>mellow</u> the tone.

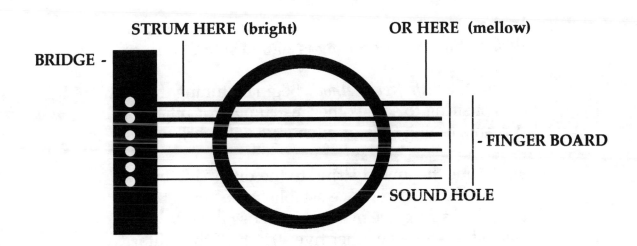

ABOUT TUNING

I. **It is vitally important that the student *memorize* the letter names and numbers of the six strings!**

II. **The preferred method of tuning the six strings of the guitar is to use an electronic tuner. These are readily available from any supplier of musical equipment and make learning to tune, as well as the ongoing task of staying in tune, much easier and far more accurate.**

III. **In the event an electronic tuner is not available, the *fifth fret method* of tuning is a good substitute.**

To use the *fifth fret method,* begin by tuning the sixth or lowest string to some other instrument or pitch source. A piano, tuning fork, or pitch pipe will work well.

First, tune the lowest string to the pitch "E" (below "middle C"). Once we've established a correct pitch for the low E string, we may begin to use the *fifth fret method* to tune the other five strings of the guitar.

To tune the fifth string (A) simply press down the sixth string at the fifth fret. The pitch you play will be A. Now turn the tuning peg for the A string and listen as the pitch of the A string either rises (counter clockwise) or falls (clockwise). When the open A string pitch matches the pitch of the sixth string at the fifth fret, the A string is in tune.

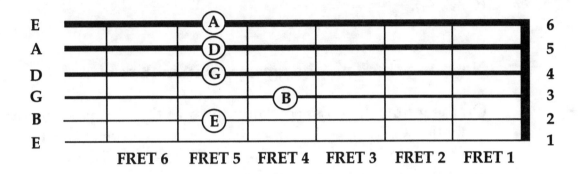

Continue this process by tuning the

D string to the fifth fret of the A string,
G string to the fifth fret of the D string,
B string to the **fourth** fret of the G string,
and the high E string to the fifth fret of the B string.

Now your instrument is in tune and *READY TO PLAY!*

ABOUT CHORD CONSTRUCTION

I.   **A chord is a combination of three or more notes played at the same time.**

The notes in the C major scale are: C, D, E, F, G, A, & B. Chords in the key of C are constructed with combinations of these notes. To make the C major chord, simply play the 1st, 3rd, and 5th notes of the C major scale at the same time (C, E, G).

II.   **Notes in a chord may be repeated within the chord.**

On the guitar the most common form of the C major chord is spelled C, E, G, C, E. This means that the notes C and E are repeated in the chord. The two Cs are one "octave," or eight notes, apart. The two Es are also eight notes apart.

Think:

C	D	**E**	F	G	A	B	**C**	D	**E**
1	2	3	4	5	6	7	**8** (1)		
		1	2	3	4	5	6	7	**8** (1)

III.   **Notes moved one half-step to the next highest position or "fret" are considered to be "sharp" (#). (See Appendix II.)**

IV.   **Notes moved one half-step to the next lowest position or "fret" are considered to be "flat" (♭). (See Appendix II.)**

ABOUT CHORD DIAGRAMS

I. CHORD DIAGRAMS

By using chord diagrams, the guitarist is able to understand where to place the left hand fingers to form a particular chord.

THE C MAJOR CHORD DIAGRAM

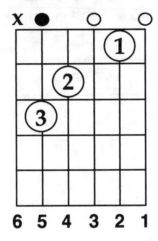

II. STRING NUMBERS

Guitar strings are numbered: 6 5 4 3 2 1

Pick up your guitar. Hold it facing you with the neck pointing up and the body hanging down (vertically). Look straight at the finger board. With the instrument in this position, the lowest string (**6**) is on the far left of the finger board and the highest string (**1**) is on the far right.

The sixth or top string is the largest string of the guitar. The first or bottom string is the smallest. To use the chord diagram, read the string numbers from left (largest) to right (smallest) in descending order:

6 5 4 3 2 1

III. FRET BARS & FRET NUMBERS

The horizontal lines on the chord diagram represent the "fret bars," which run from left to right across the guitar finger board.

Between two fret bars is a fret. The frets are numbered in ascending order beginning with the first fret (at the top next to the "nut") and ending with the last fret (at the bottom of the finger board next to the sound hole).

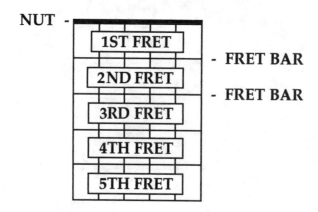

IV. FINGER POSITION MARKERS—②

The large circles placed on the vertical lines of the chord diagram are finger position markers. These tell where to place each left hand finger for any given chord.

The left hand fingers of the guitarist are numbered:

T (thumb), 1 (index), 2 (middle), 3 (ring), and 4 (pinky).

The C Major chord diagram indicates the following:

1. Place the first finger (index) on the second string in the first fret.
2. Place the second finger (middle) on the fourth string in the second fret.
3. Place the third finger (ring) on the fifth string in the third fret.

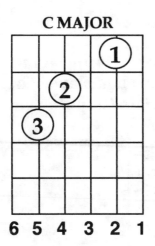

- FIRST FRET FINGER POSITION

- SECOND FRET FINGER POSITION

- THIRD FRET FINGER POSITION

V.   BASS (ROOT) NOTE INDICATORS—●

A small black circle placed over a string at the top of the chord diagram indicates the "bass" or "root" note of the chord. This is the lowest note in the chord and usually has the same name as the chord.

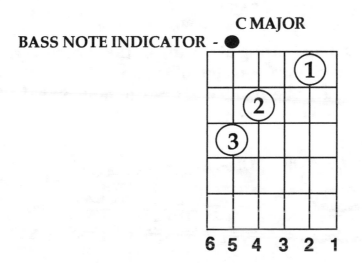

The C Major chord is built on the bass or root note C. Therefore, in the C Major chord diagram, ● = the bass note, C.

VI.   OPEN STRING INDICATORS—○

A small open circle placed over a string at the top of the chord diagram indicates that the string is played "open," with no left hand finger pressing it down or "stopping" it.

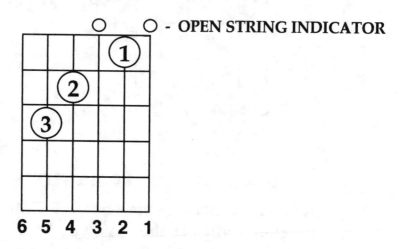

VII.   DO NOT PLAY INDICATOR—x

An x placed over a string at the top of the chord diagram indicates that the string is not to be played in that chord. The string must either be avoided entirely or muted by the light touch of a left hand finger.

DO NOT PLAY INDICATOR - X

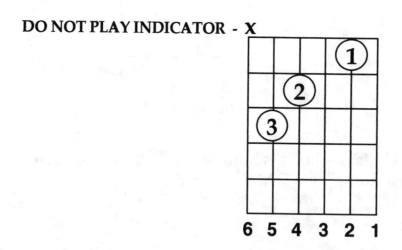

II. THE KEY OF C MAJOR

CHORD DIAGRAM REVIEW

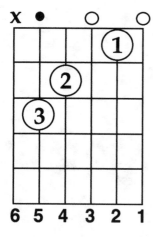   = C MAJOR CHORD DIAGRAM

X   X   = DO NOT PLAY INDICATORS

●   ●   ●   = BASS OR ROOT NOTE INDICATORS

○   ○   ○   = OPEN STRING INDICATORS

①   ②   ③   ④   = FINGER POSITION MARKERS

6 5 4 3 2 1   = STRING NUMBERS

CHORDS IN THE KEY OF C MAJOR

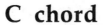

Key of C **CHORD NAME**:	**C**	Dm	Em	**F**	**G**	Am	Bdim	**C**
SCALE DEGREE NUMBER[1] :	**I**	II	III	**IV**	**V**	VI	VII	**I**

C chord

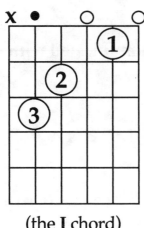

(the **I** chord)

F chord[2]

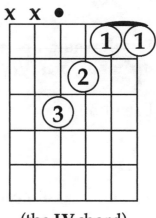

(the **IV** chord)

G chord

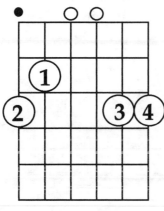

(the **V** chord)

G7 chord

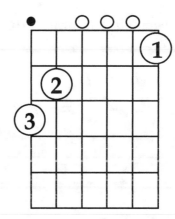

(a substitute for the G chord[3])

---

[1] See APPENDIX I, THE NUMBER SYSTEM

[2] ▬▬▬ = "barre" chord (use first finger to press down the first *and* second strings)

[3] Because G7 is easier to play than G, the student may choose to begin by substituting the G7 for the G chord.

ABOUT PLAYING CHORDS

I.   **A guitarist plays "rhythm guitar" by strumming chords.**

 ⊓ = **down strum**   V = **up strum**

II.   **Rhythm guitar parts are often communicated with simple diagonal lines: / / / /.**

Each line represents one beat.   / / / /
                                  1 2 3 4

III. **The number of beats per measure of music is determined by the top number of the time signature:**

$$\frac{4}{4} = \text{four (4) beats per measure}$$

For each measure count steadily: **one, two, three, four**.

$\frac{4}{4}$ / / / /   / / / /   / / / /   / / / /
    1 2 3 4   1 2 3 4   1 2 3 4   1 2 3 4

$$\frac{3}{4} = \text{three (3) beats per measure}$$

For each measure count steadily: **one, two, three**.

$\frac{3}{4}$ / / /   / / /   / / /   / / /
    1 2 3   1 2 3   1 2 3   1 2 3

THE C MAJOR CHORD

C chord

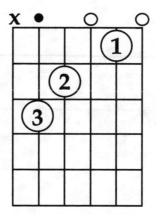

(the I chord in the key of C)

Play the C chord, strumming steadily down, down, down, down (⊓⊓⊓⊓).

$\frac{4}{4}$ C   C   C   C

/ / / /   / / / /   / / / /   / / / /

1 2 3 4

Play the C chord, strumming steadily down, down, down (⊓⊓⊓).

$\frac{3}{4}$ C   C   C   C

/ / /   / / /   / / /   / / /

1 2 3

Play the C chord, strumming steadily down, up, down, up (⊓V⊓V).

$\frac{4}{4}$ C   C   C   C

/ / / /   / / / /   / / / /   / / / /

THE G MAJOR CHORD

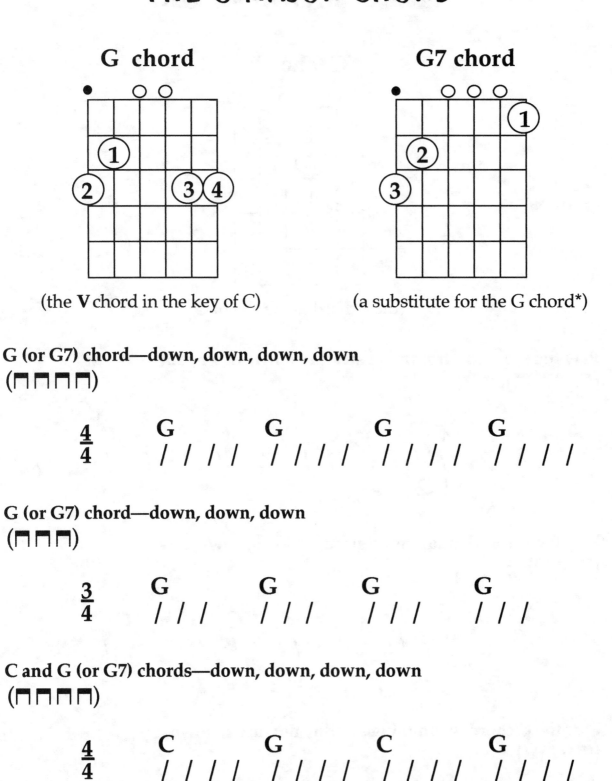

G chord

(the **V** chord in the key of C)

G7 chord

(a substitute for the G chord*)

G (or G7) chord—down, down, down, down
(⊓ ⊓ ⊓ ⊓)

$\frac{4}{4}$ G   G   G   G
/ / / /   / / / /   / / / /   / / / /

G (or G7) chord—down, down, down
(⊓ ⊓ ⊓)

$\frac{3}{4}$ G   G   G   G
/ / /   / / /   / / /   / / /

C and G (or G7) chords—down, down, down, down
(⊓ ⊓ ⊓ ⊓)

$\frac{4}{4}$ C   G   C   G
/ / / /   / / / /   / / / /   / / / /

* Because G7 is easier to play than G, the student may choose to begin by substituting the G7 for the G chord.

THE F MAJOR CHORD

F chord*

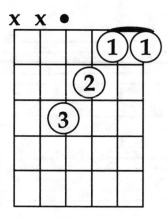

(the **IV** chord in the key of C)

F chord

⊓ ⊓ ⊓ ⊓ *or* ⊓ V ⊓ V

$\frac{4}{4}$ F / / / /   F / / / /   F / / / /   F / / / /

F chord

⊓ ⊓ ⊓

$\frac{3}{4}$ F / / /   F / / /   F / / /   F / / /

C, F, and G chords

⊓ ⊓ ⊓ ⊓ *or* ⊓ V ⊓ V

$\frac{4}{4}$ C / / / /   F / / / /   G / / / /   C / / / /

* ⏜ = "barre" chord (use first finger to press down the first *and* second strings)

EXERCISE 1
STRUM: ⊓⊓⊓⊓

♩ = 84 (a tempo marking which indicates to play at 84 beats per minute—see APPENDIX IV.)

* ◇ = strum once and hold the chord for 2 beats.

** ◇ = strum once and hold the chord for 4 beats.

EXERCISE 2
STRUM: ⊓⊓⊓

♩ = 100   (a tempo marking which indicates to play at 100 beats per minute—see **APPENDIX IV**.)

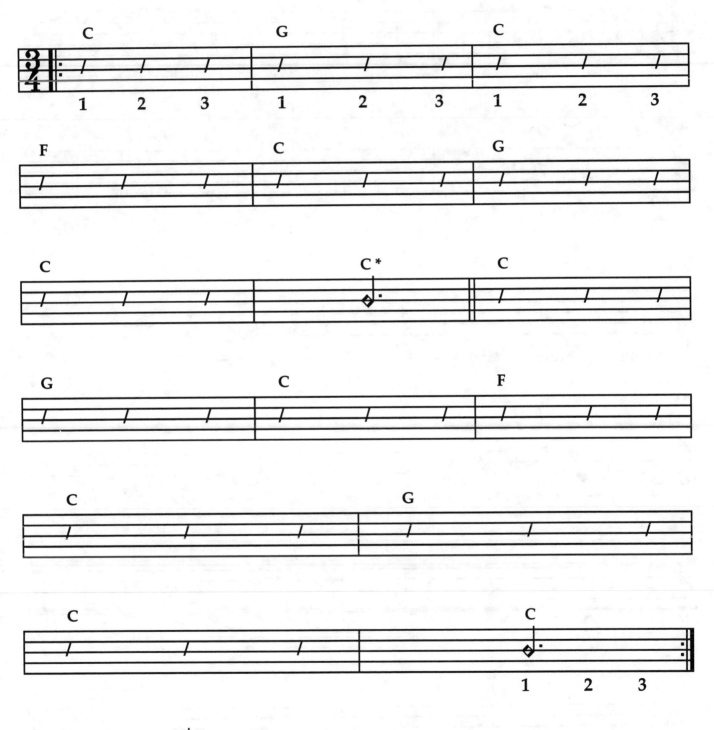

* ◊• = **strum once and hold the chord for 3 beats**

THEY'RE FOR YOU—Key of C

STRUM: ⊓ ⊓ ⊓ ⊓

Samuel Hoffman

III. THE KEY OF G MAJOR

CHORD DIAGRAM REVIEW

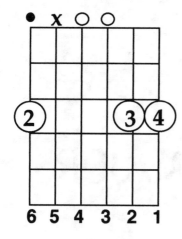

= Gno3 CHORD DIAGRAM

= BASS or ROOT NOTE INDICATORS

= DO NOT PLAY INDICATORS

= OPEN STRING INDICATORS

= FINGER POSITION MARKERS

6 5 4 3 2 1   = STRING NUMBERS

CHORDS IN THE KEY OF G MAJOR

Key of G **CHORD NAME:**	**G**	A m	Bm	**C**	**D**	Em	F#dim	**G**
SCALE DEGREE NUMBER:	**I**	II	III	**IV**	**V**	VI	VII	**I**

Gno3 chord

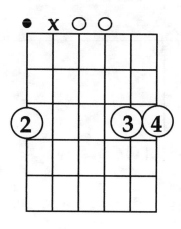

(the **I** chord)

Cadd9 chord

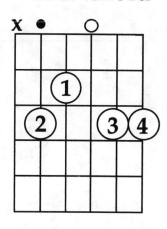

(the **IV** chord)

D4 chord

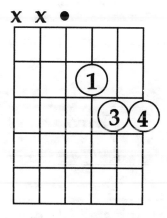

(the **V** chord)

THE Gno3 CHORD

Gno3

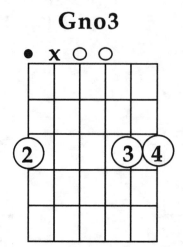

(the I chord in the key of G)

Play the Gno3 chord, strumming steadily down, down, down, down (⊓⊓⊓⊓).

$\frac{4}{4}$ Gno3   Gno3   Gno3   Gno3
    / / / /   / / / /   / / / /   / / / /

Play the Gno3 chord, strumming steadily down, down, down (⊓⊓⊓).

$\frac{3}{4}$ Gno3   Gno3   Gno3   Gno3
    / / /   / / /   / / /   / / /

Play the Gno3 chord, strumming steadily down, up, down, up (⊓∨⊓∨).

$\frac{4}{4}$ Gno3   Gno3   Gno3   Gno3
    / / / /   / / / /   / / / /   / / / /

THE Cadd9 CHORD

Cadd9

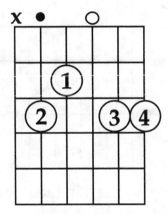

(the **IV** chord in the key of G)

Cadd9 chord—down, down, down, down
(⊓ ⊓ ⊓ ⊓)

$\frac{4}{4}$ **Cadd9**   **Cadd9**   **Cadd9**   **Cadd9**
/ / / /   / / / /   / / / /   / / / /

Cadd9 chord—down, down, down
(⊓ ⊓ ⊓)

$\frac{3}{4}$ **Cadd9**   **Cadd9**   **Cadd9**   **Cadd9**
/ / /   / / /   / / /   / / /

Gno3 and Cadd9 chords—down, up, down, up
(⊓ V ⊓ V)

$\frac{4}{4}$ **Gno3**   **Cadd9**   **Gno3**   **Cadd9**
/ / / /   / / / /   / / / /   / / / /

(repeat the line)

THE D4 CHORD

D4

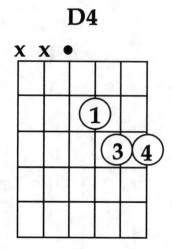

(the V chord in the key of G)

D4 chord

⊓ ⊓ ⊓ ⊓ *or* ⊓ V ⊓ V

$\frac{4}{4}$ **D 4** / / / /   **D4** / / / /   **D 4** / / / /   **D 4** / / / /

D4 chord

⊓ ⊓ ⊓

$\frac{3}{4}$ **D 4** / / /   **D4** / / /   **D 4** / / /   **D4** / / /

Gno3, Cadd9, and D4 chords

⊓ V ⊓ V

$\frac{4}{4}$ **Gno3** / / / /   **Cadd9** / / / /   **D4** / / / /   **Cadd9** / / / / :‖

(repeat the line)

EXERCISE 3
STRUM: ⊓V⊓V

♩ = 84

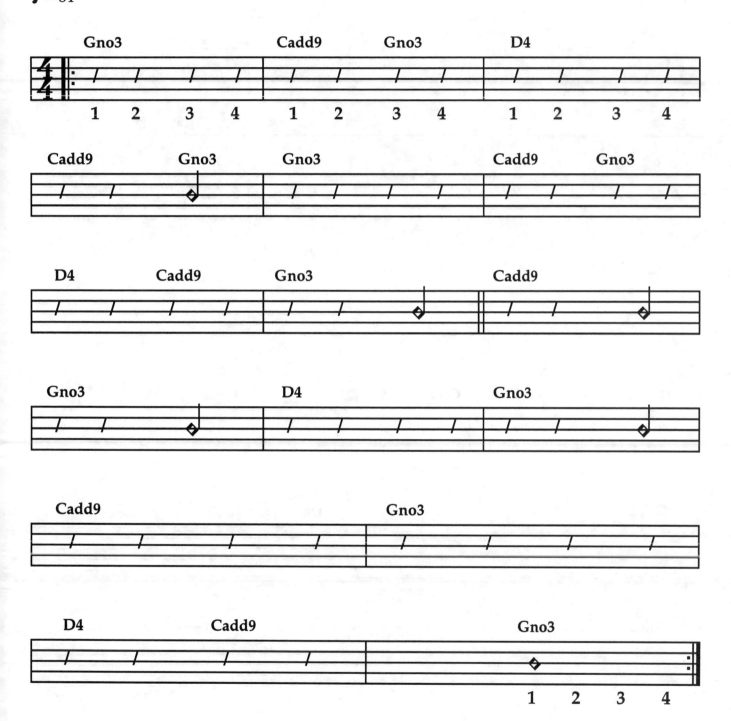

EXERCISE 4

STRUM: ⊓∨⊓

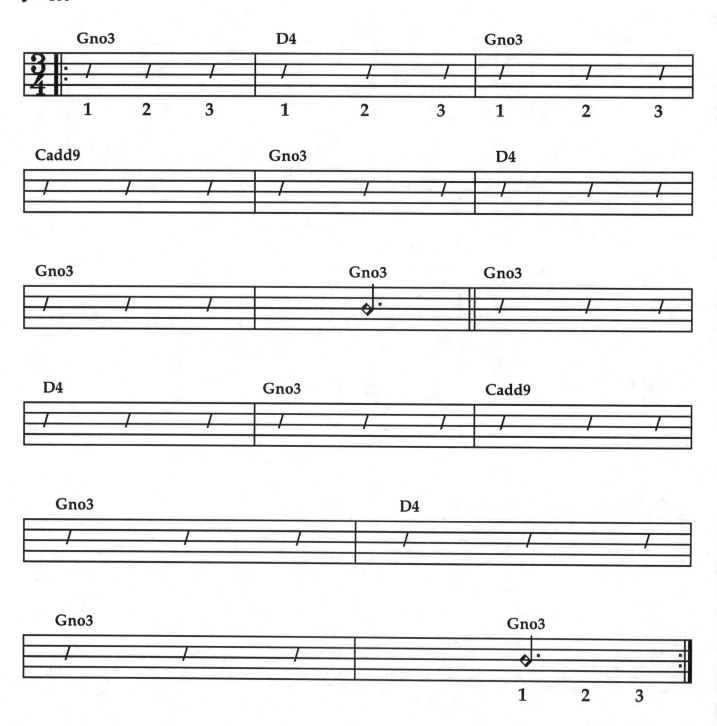

I GIVE YOU EVERYTHING

STRUM:

Samuel Hoffman

YOUR NOTES:

♪♪ ♩ ♩ ♪♪

IV. THE KEY OF D MAJOR

CHORDS IN THE KEY OF D MAJOR

Key of D **CHORD NAME**:	**D**	Em	F#m	**G**	**A**	Bm	C#dim	**D**
SCALE DEGREE NUMBER:	**I**	II	III	**IV**	**V**	VI	VII	**I**

D chord

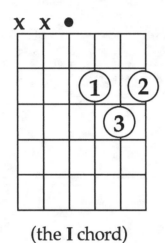

(the **I** chord)

G chord

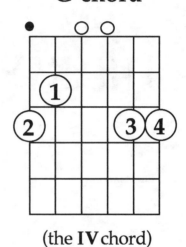

(the **IV** chord)

A chord

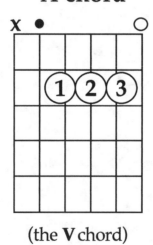

(the **V** chord)

x = do not play   o = play open   ● = root (bass) note

THE D MAJOR CHORD

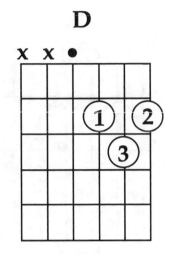

(the **I** chord in the key of D)

Play the D chord, strumming steadily down, down, down, down (⊓⊓⊓⊓).

$\frac{4}{4}$ D   / / / /   D   / / / /   D   / / / /   D   / / / /

Play the D chord, strumming steadily down, down, down (⊓⊓⊓).

$\frac{3}{4}$ D   / / /   D   / / /   D   / / /   D   / / /

Play the D chord, strumming steadily down, up, down, up (⊓∨⊓∨).

$\frac{4}{4}$ D   / / / /   D   / / / /   D   / / / /   D   / / / /

THE G MAJOR CHORD

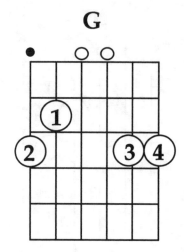

G

(the **IV** chord in the key of D)

G chord—down, down, down, down
(⊓ ⊓ ⊓ ⊓)

$\frac{4}{4}$　　**G**　　　　　**G**　　　　　**G**　　　　　**G**
　　　　/ / / /　　/ / / /　　/ / / /　　/ / / /

G and D chords—down, up, down
(⊓ ∨ ⊓)

play at / = **100,** which means the tempo is 100 beats per minute (see
APPENDIX IV.)

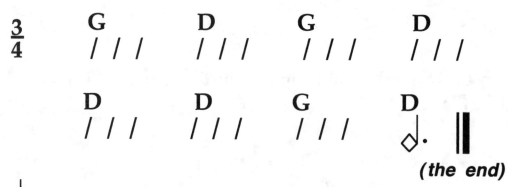

$\frac{3}{4}$　**G**　　　**D**　　　**G**　　　**D**
　　/ / /　　/ / /　　/ / /　　/ / /

　　D　　　**D**　　　**G**　　　**D**
　　/ / /　　/ / /　　/ / /　　♩. ‖

　　　　　　　　　　　　　　　(the end)

♩. = strum once and hold the chord for 3 beats

-34-

THE A MAJOR CHORD

A

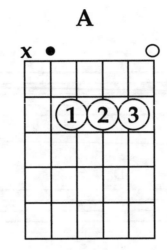

(the **V** chord in the key of D)

A chord
⊓ ⊓ ⊓ ⊓ *or* ⊓ V ⊓ V

$\frac{4}{4}$ A   A   A   A
/ / / /   / / / /   / / / /   / / / /

A chord
⊓ V ⊓

$\frac{3}{4}$ A   A   A   A
/ / /   / / /   / / /   / / /

D, G, and A chords (/ = 140)
⊓ ⊓ ⊓ ⊓ *or* ⊓ V ⊓ V

$\frac{4}{4}$ D   G   A   A
/ / / /   / / / /   / / / /   / / / / :||

(repeat the line)

EXERCISE 5
STRUM: ⊓V⊓V

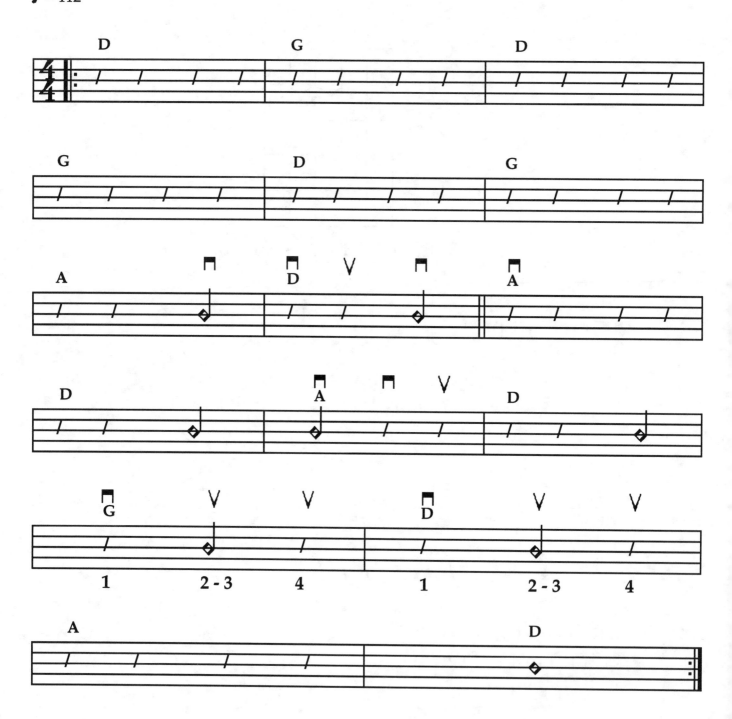

EXERCISE 6
STRUM: ⊓⊓⊓⊓

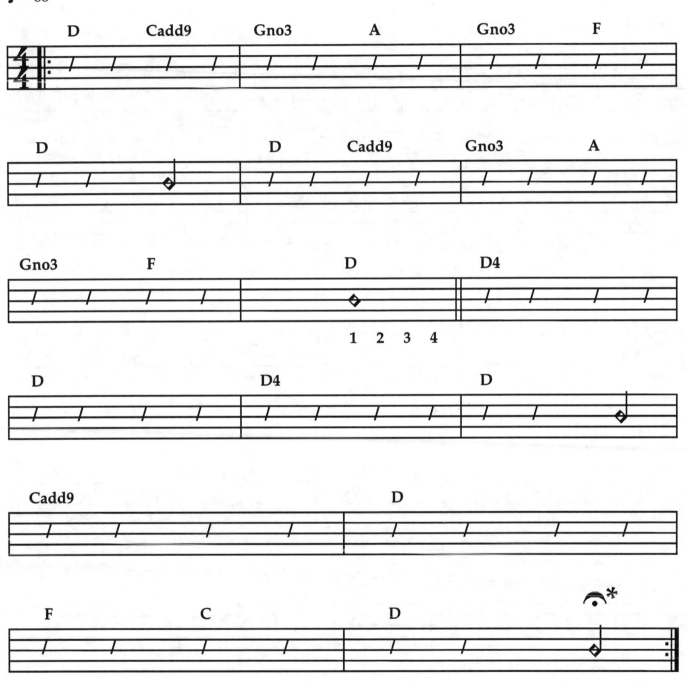

* ◠• = strum once and hold the chord extra long

LORD, YOU'RE GOOD—Key of D

STRUM: ⊓⊓⊓⊓

Samuel Hoffman

THEY'RE FOR YOU—Key of D

STRUM: ⊓⊓⊓⊓

Samuel Hoffman

YOUR NOTES: ♪♪ ♩ ♩ ♪♪

_____

_____

_____

_____

_____

_____

_____

_____

V. THE KEY OF E MAJOR

CHORDS IN THE KEY OF E MAJOR

Key of E **CHORD NAME:**	E	F#m	G#m	A	B	C#m	D#dim	E
SCALE DEGREE NUMBER:	I	II	III	IV	V	VI	VII	I

E chord

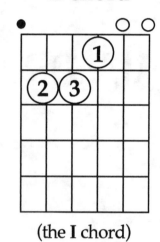

(the **I** chord)

A2 chord

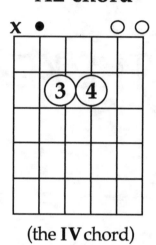

(the **IV** chord)

B4 chord

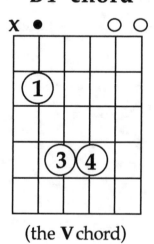

(the **V** chord)

x = do not play   o = play open   ● = root (bass) note

THE E MAJOR CHORD

E

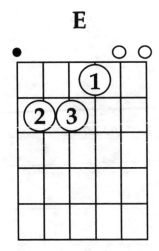

(the I chord in the key of E)

Play the E chord, strumming steadily down, down, down, down (⊓ ⊓ ⊓ ⊓).

/ = 112

$\frac{4}{4}$ E / / / / E / / / / E / / / / E / / / /

Strum the E chord—down, up, down, up, down, up, down, up (⊓V ⊓V ⊓V ⊓V).

1 & 2 & 3 & 4 &*

/ = 88

$\frac{4}{4}$ E / / / / E / / / / E / / / / E / / / /

E / / / / E / / / / E / / / / E / / / /

* This is an "eighth note" rhythm. Play two strums (⊓V) for each beat or /.

THE A2 CHORD

A2

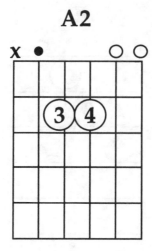

(the **IV** chord in the key of E)

A2 chord
down, down - up, down / down, down - up, down

⊓	⊓	V	⊓		⊓	⊓	V	⊓
1	2	&	3		1	2	&	3*

/ = **108**

$\frac{3}{4}$

A2	A2	A2	A2
/ / /	/ / /	/ / /	/ / /
1 2& 3	1 2& 3	1 2& 3	1 2& 3

A2	A2	A2	A2
/ / /	/ / /	/ / /	♩. ‖

♩. = **strum once and hold the chord for 3 beats**

* This is an eighth note rhythm. The second beat of each measure is divided into
   two equal parts and played down, up (⊓V).

THE B4 CHORD

B 4

(the **V** chord in the key of E)

B4 chord

⊓ ⊓ ⊓ ⊓ *or* ⊓ V ⊓ V

$\frac{4}{4}$ **B4**   **B4**   **B4**   **B4**

/ / / /   / / / /   / / / /   / / / /

E, A2, and B4 chords

⊓ ⊓ ⊓ ⊓ *or* ⊓ V ⊓ V

$\frac{4}{4}$ **B4**   **A2**   **B4**   **A2**

/ / / /   / / / /   / / / /   / / / /

B4   **A2**   **E**   **E**

/ / / /   / / / /   / / / /   / / / /

A2 B4 E   **A2 B4**   **E**

/ / / /   / / / /   / / / /   ◇   :||

◇ = **strum once and hold the chord for 4 beats**

EXERCISE 7
STRUM: ⊓⊓⊓⊓

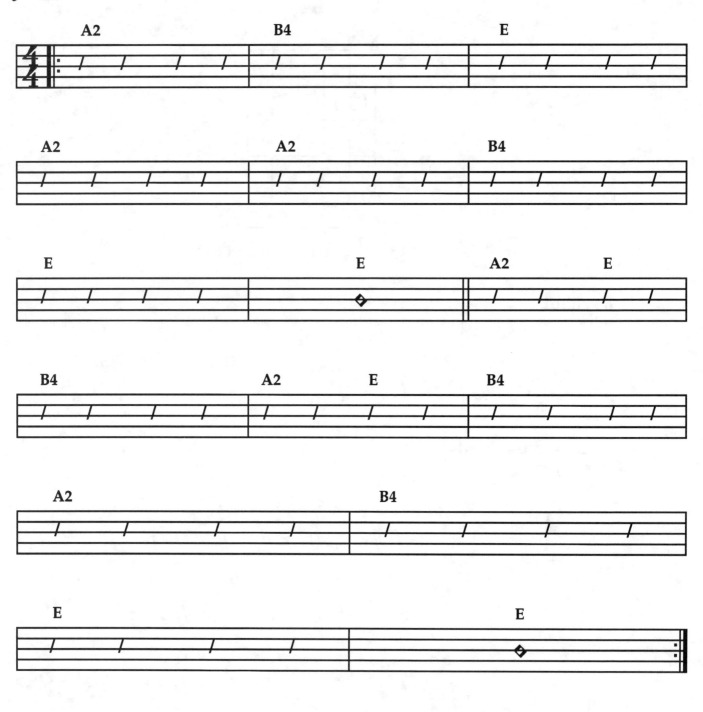

◇ = strum once and hold the chord for 4 beats

EXERCISE 8

STRUM: ⊓V⊓

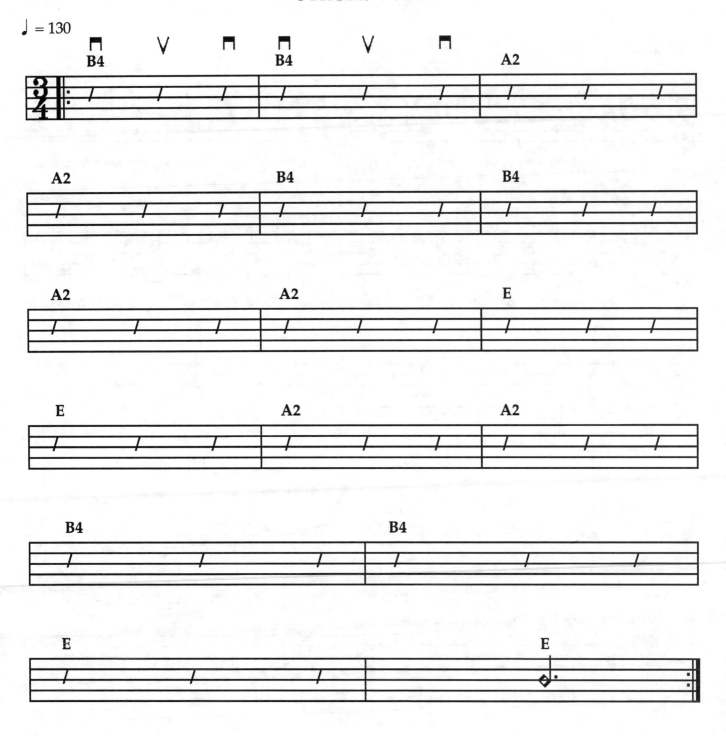

◇. = strum once and hold the chord for 3 beats

LORD, YOU'RE GOOD—Key of E

STRUM: ⊓⊓⊓⊓

Samuel Hoffman

♩ = 106

CHORUS:

| A2 | E | B4 | E | A2 | E |

Lord, You're good— and Your mer-cy — en-dures Lord, You're good and Your

| B4 | E | A2 | E | B4 | E |

mer-cy — en-dures Lord You're good— and Your mer-cy — en-dures for-ev —

| A2 | B4 | A2 | E |

— er — and ev — er — Lord, You're good— and Your

| B4 | E | A2 | E | B4 | E |

mer-cy — en-dures Lord, You're good and Your mer-cy — en-dures

| A2 | E | B4 | E | A2 |

Lord, You're good- and Your mer-cy — en-dures for- ev — er —

| A2 | E | (REST) |

and ev — er — .

THEY'RE FOR YOU—Key of E

STRUM:

Samuel Hoffman

Beginning Worship Guitar

YOUR NOTES:

♪♪ ♩ ♩ ♪♪

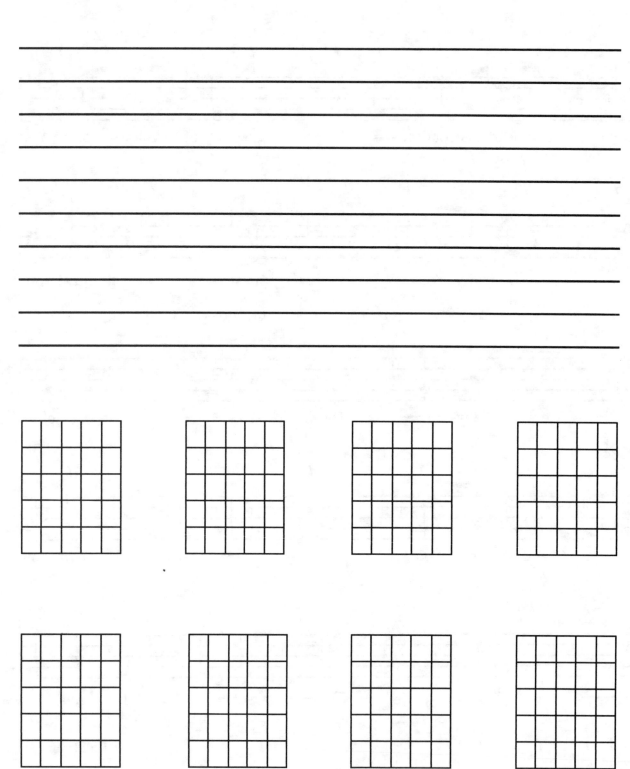

VI. MINOR KEYS

CHORDS IN THE KEY OF A MINOR

I.　　Each major key has a relative minor key. This means that they are kin to each other because they share a "key signature." They both have the same number of sharps and flats. (See page 6.)

II.　　To determine the relative minor key of any major key, simply step backwards down the musical alphabet one and one-half steps: C Major - B - B♭ - A Minor.

III.　　The key of A Minor is relative to the key of C Major. They both have *no* sharps or flats.

Key of Am **CHORD NAME:**	**Am**	Bm	C	**Dm**	E	F	G	**Am**
SCALE DEGREE NUMBER:	**I**	II	III	**IV**	**V**	VI	VII	**I**

Am chord

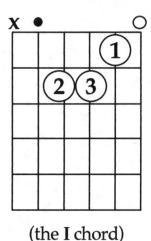

(the **I** chord)

Dm chord

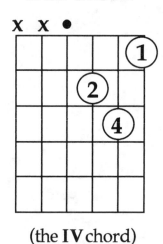

(the **IV** chord)

E chord

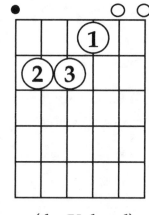

(the **V** chord)

x = do not play　　　　　　O = play open　　　　　　● = root (bass) note

THE A Minor CHORD

A m

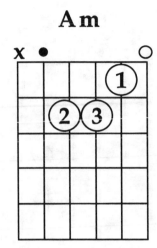

(the **I** chord in the key of Am)

Play the Am chord, strumming steadily down, down, down, down
(⊓ ⊓ ⊓ ⊓).

◢ = 112

$\frac{4}{4}$ | Am / / / / | Am / / / / | Am / / / / | Am / / / / |

Strum the Am chord—down, up, down, up, down, up, down, up
(⊓∨ ⊓∨ ⊓∨ ⊓∨).

1 & 2 & 3 & 4 &

◢ = 96

$\frac{4}{4}$ | Am / / / / | Am / / / / | Am / / / / | Am / / / / |

| Am / / / / | Am / / / / | Am / / / / | Am / / / / |

THE D Minor CHORD

Dm

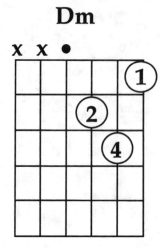

(the **IV** chord in the key of Am)

Dm chord

down, down - up, down / down, down - up, down

⊓	⊓	V	⊓	⊓	⊓	V	⊓
1	2	&	3	1	2	&	3

/ = 112

$\frac{3}{4}$

Dm	Dm	Dm	Dm
/ / /	/ / /	/ / /	/ / /
1 2& 3	1 2& 3	1 2& 3	1 2& 3

Dm	Dm	Dm	Dm
/ / /	/ / /	/ / /	◊. ▌▌

◊. = strum once and hold the chord for 3 beats

PLAY ALL THREE
(Am, Dm, E)

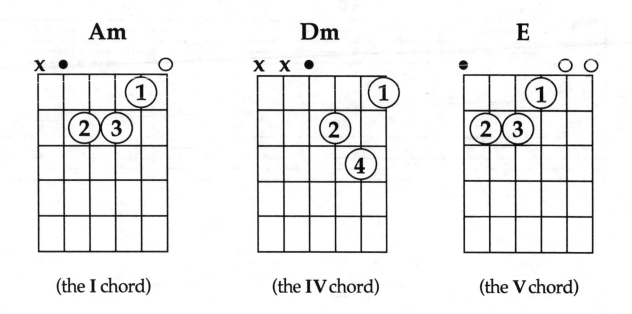

Am (the I chord)   Dm (the IV chord)   E (the V chord)

Am, Dm, and E chords

down, down - up, down / down, down - up, down

⊓ ⊓ ∨ ⊓ ⊓ ⊓ ∨ ⊓

1 2 & 3 1 2 & 3

♩ = 108

3/4	Am / / /	Dm / / /	E / / /	Am / / /
	1 2& 3	1 2& 3	1 2& 3	1 2& 3
	Am / / /	Dm / / /	E / / /	Am ♩.

EXERCISE 9

STRUM: ⊓⊓⊓⊓ *or* ⊓∨⊓∨

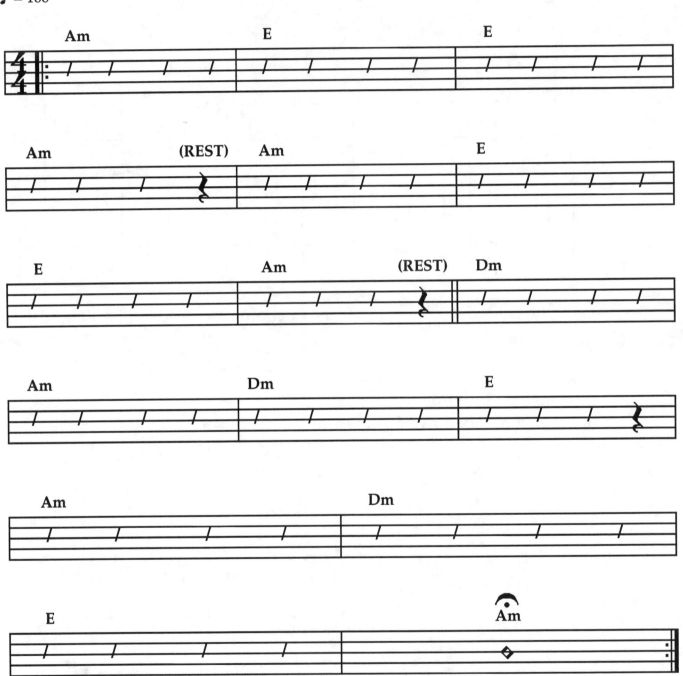

CHORDS IN THE KEY OF E MINOR

I.   To determine the relative minor key of a major, simply step backwards down the musical alphabet one and one-half steps: G Major - G♭ - F - E Minor.

II.   The key of E Minor is relative to the key of G Major. They both have *one* sharp.

Key of Em **CHORD NAME:**	Em	F#m	G	**Am**	**B**	C	D	**Em**
SCALE DEGREE NUMBER:	**I**	II	III	**IV**	**V**	VI	VII	**I**

Em chord

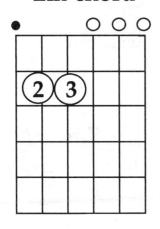

(the **I** chord)

Am chord

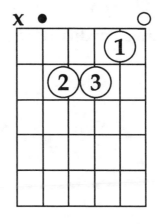

(the **IV** chord)

B4 chord

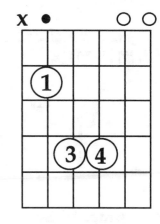

(the **V** chord)

x = do not play   O = play open   ● = root (bass) note

THE E Minor CHORD

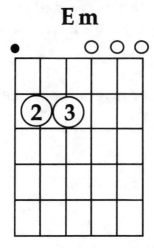

(the **I** chord in the key of Em)

Play the Em chord, strumming steadily down, down, down, down
(⊓ ⊓ ⊓ ⊓).

/ = 112

4/4 Em / / / / Em / / / / Em / / / / Em / / / /

Em, Am, and B4 chords
(⊓V ⊓V ⊓V ⊓V)
 1 & 2 & 3 & 4 &

/ = 126

4/4 Am / / / / Em / / / / B4 / / / / Em / / / /

Am / / / / Em / / / / B4 / / / / Em ◇ :‖

A SENSE OF PLACE

STRUM: ⊓ (unless otherwise indicated).

♩ = 72

Samuel Hoffman

Fine (the end)

d.c. al Fine *

* d.c. al Fine = go back to the beginning and play until you reach **Fine (the end)**

YOUR NOTES:

♪♪ ♩ ♩ ♪♪

VII. ALL TOGETHER NOW!

CHORDS:
CLEAN HANDS AND A PURE HEART

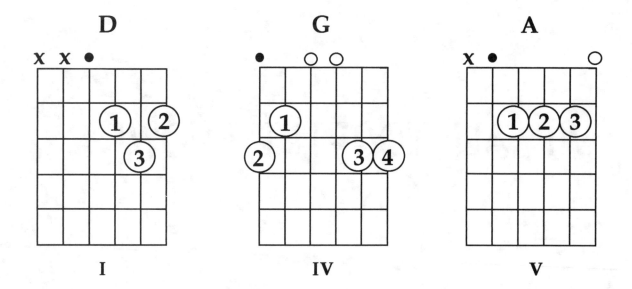

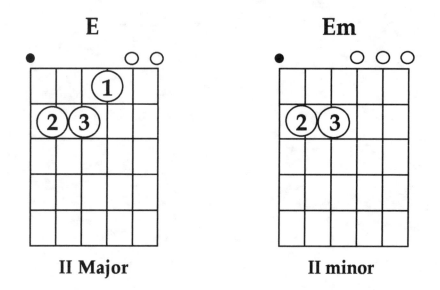

x = do not play   O = play open   ● = root (bass) note

CLEAN HANDS AND A PURE HEART

STRUM: ⊓⊓⊓⊓

Samuel Hoffman

CHORDS:
FULFILL OUR LONGING

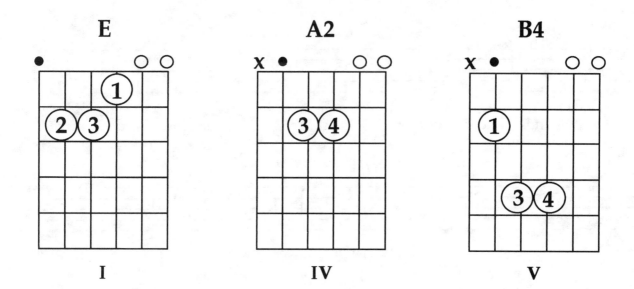

A NEW CHORD:

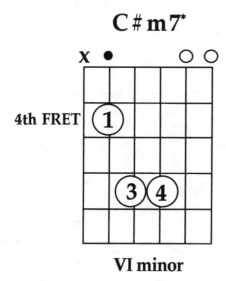

* To play the C#m7 chord, simply use the B4 chord fingering and slide the left hand up the finger board 2 frets. The 1st finger will then be located in the 4th fret.

x = do not play   **o** = play open   ● = root (bass) note

FULFILL OUR LONGING

STRUM: ⊓V ⊓V ⊓V ⊓V
1 & 2 & 3 & 4 &

♩ = 77

Samuel Hoffman

CHORUS

E · E · A2 · B4
O, Lord ———, Ful - fill our long -ing for You

E · A2 · B4 · C#m7
Lord ———, You know we're long-ing for Your touch the sound of Your voice-

B4 · A2 · E · A2 · B4
— the beat of Your heart — chang- ing our lives — ful- fill our

E · E · (HOLD)
long - ing

CHORDS:
TAKE ME THERE

Gno3   ### Cadd9   ### D4

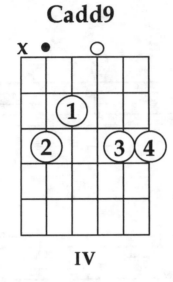

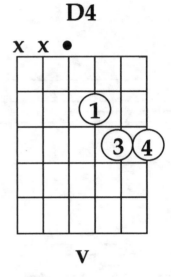

I   IV   V

A NEW CHORD:

A7

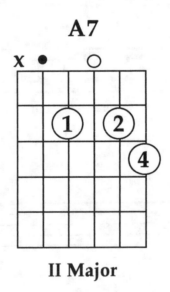

II Major

x = do not play   ○ = play open   ● = root (bass) note

TAKE ME THERE

STRUM: ⊓ ⊓ ⊓ ⊓

Samuel Hoffman

♩ = 140

YOUR NOTES:

♪♪ ♩ ♩ ♪♪

APPENDICES

THE NUMBER SYSTEM

The Number System (reference page 13) is a system which is used to communicate and cross reference chord progressions.

I. **A chord progression is a series of chords played in a predetermined sequence.**

Chord:	C	F	G	C	C	F	G	C
Beat Number:	**1,2**	**3,4**	**1,2**	**3,4**	**1,2**	**3,4**	**1,2**	**3,4**

II. **In addition to calling chords by their letter names, C, F, G, and so on, chords can be identified by numbers. For instance, in the key of C, the C chord is chord number I. Starting with C and counting four up the scale to F makes F the number IV chord and G the number V chord.**

Chord:	C	D	E	F	G	A	B	C
Chord Number:	**I**	**II**	**III**	**IV**	**V**	**VI**	**VII**	**I**

III. **Now instead of calling it the "C, F, G" chord progression we can identify it as the "I, IV, V" chord progression.**

Chord:	C	F	G	C	C	F	G	C
Chord Number:	**I**	**IV**	**V**	**I**	**I**	**IV**	**V**	**I**
Beat Number:	**1,2**	**3,4**	**1,2**	**3,4**	**1,2**	**3,4**	**1,2**	**3,4**

IV. **It is easy to recognize the benefit of communicating with the number system. If we use numbers instead of letters to indicate chord progressions, we are then free to use the same chord progression in as many different keys as we like without ever having to rewrite the music.**

Number:	**I**	**IV**	**V**	**I**		**I**	**IV**	**V**	**I**
Chord:	C	F	G	C		C	F	G	C
	G	C	D	G		G	C	D	G
	D	G	A	D		D	G	A	D
	E	A	B	E		E	A	B	E

THE KEYS

The Cycle of 5ths: There is an interval of a fifth (3 1/2 steps) between each of the following keys.

key of **C** to key of **G** example:	**C**	**D**	**E**	**F**	**G**
count up the scale:	**1**	**2**	**3**	**4**	**5**

Using the *cycle of 5ths* (beginning with the key of C) will help you to remember the key names and number of sharps or flats in each.

<u>KEY</u>	<u>NUMBER OF SHARPS (#) or FLATS (♭)</u>	
C	**0** sharps or flats	
G	**1** sharp	(F#)
D	**2** sharps	(F#, C#)
A	**3** sharps	(F#, C#, G#)
E	**4** sharps	(F#, C#, G#, D#)
B (C♭—7 flats)	**5** sharps	(F#, C#, G#, D#, A#)
F# (G♭—6 flats)	**6** sharps	(F#, C#, G#, D#, A#, E#)
C# (D♭—5 flats)	**7** sharps	(F#, C#, G#, D#, A#, E#, B#)
A♭	**4** flats	(B♭, E♭, A♭, D♭)
E♭	**3** flats	(B♭, E♭, A♭)
B♭	**2** flats	(B♭, E♭)
F	**1** flat	(B♭)

GUITAR FINGER BOARD NOTES

String Number :	6	5	4	3	2	1
Open String Name:	E	A	D	G	B	E
fret number 1	F	A#	D#	G#	C	F
fret number 2	F#	B	E	A	C#	F#
fret number 3	G	C	F	A#	D	G
fret number 4	G#	C#	F#	B	D#	G#
fret number 5	A	D	G	C	E	A
fret number 6	A#	D#	G#	C#	F	A#
fret number 7	B	E	A	D	F#	B
fret number 8	C	F	A#	D#	G	C
fret number 9	C#	F#	B	E	G#	C#
fret number 10	D	G	C	F	A	D
fret number 11	D#	G#	C#	F#	A#	D#
fret number 12	E	A	D	G	B	E

THE METRONOME

(tempo markings)

I.   THE METRONOME (see page 18) is a device (mechanical or electronic) which clicks in perfect, steady time and allows the musician to practice without missing a beat. Tempo markings or "metronome settings" will be notated as:

note = number of beats *or* slash = number of beats

   ♩ = 100   / = 100

II.   The note or the slash represents one beat. The number (from 0 to 200) represents the number of beats per minute. / = 100 means that the speed of the song or exercise is 100 beats per minute. Simply set your metronome to 100 and it will click 100 steady times per minute. This will give you a reference for developing a sense of consistent rhythm on your instrument.

IN CLOSING

Mission Statement
The mission of Worship Works! is to honor and glorify God with contemporary praise and worship by reaching out to the unsaved and leading the saved into the presence of the Almighty.

Foundational Scripture
"For we are His workmanship, created in Christ Jesus for good works, which God prepared beforehand that we should walk in them."

Ephesians 2:10

Questions?
E-mail: essentialworship@aol.com
Website: www.worshipworksmusic.com

"because worship is essential"